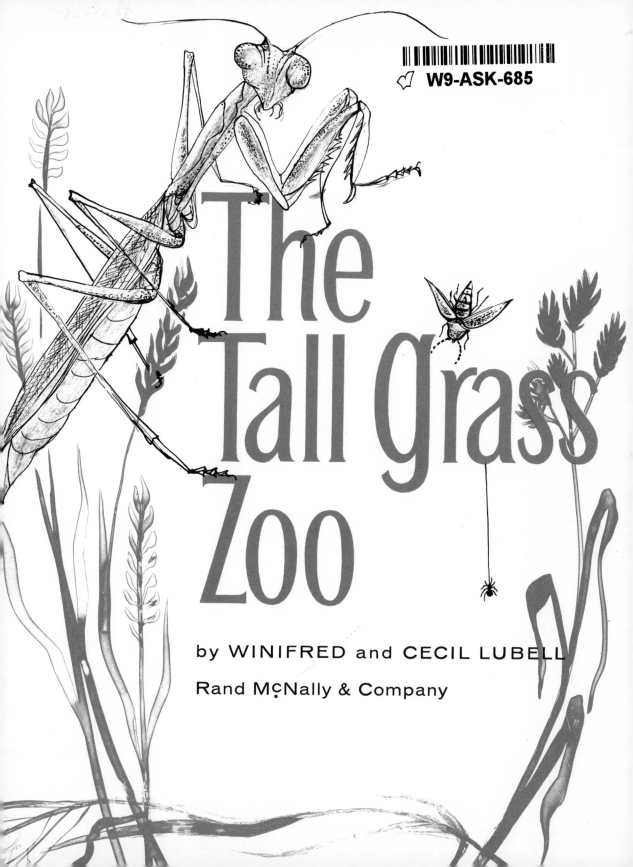

The Tall Grass Zoo

by WINIFRED and CECIL LUBELL

Rand McNally & Company

This is the Tall Grass Zoo.

It has no camels from the hot desert,
No tigers from the jungle,
No lions from the African plains,
No cages, no fences, no keepers.

In the Tall Grass Zoo
You can touch all the animals.
You can lift them up.
You can hold them carefully in your hand.
You can examine them with a magnifying
   glass
Before you put them gently down
To scurry away among the leaves and
   grass.
The Tall Grass Zoo is your own back yard.

Here is a whole new world for you to
  explore—
A world full of tiny living things.
So many of them,
There are more than all the people of the
  earth
Many times over.
Creatures so small
You can stand like a giant over them . . .

A wonderful world full of many wonders.

A quiet world, too.
You must stand very still,
Walk very lightly,
Be gentle and kind
To the creatures you find.
You must know where to look
And how to look sharp . . .
Under the leaves,
In the tall, tall grass,
On the bark of trees,
Among the rocks and the earth.
Let us go and look. . . .

THE DADDY LONGLEGS

The longest legs for a spider his size

Belong to the creature whose first name is *Daddy*.
His last name is *Longlegs*, as everyone
    knows.
The Daddy Longlegs has eight legs in all.
And if he should lose one,
Or break one while running,
He grows back a new one within a short
    while—
Just as *you* grow front teeth.

You need not be frightened of a Daddy
    Longlegs.
He won't ever hurt you,
Or sting you or bite,
And he's great fun to watch.

If you put out some food
You may see how he eats.
He sticks one long leg right into the dish
And then licks it clean.

THE BUTTERFLY

Everyone knows the elephant
Has a trunk like a vacuum cleaner.
He uses it for drinking
And sometimes to give himself a shower.

The *Butterfly* also has a trunk.
It's not quite the same
But it's used the same way.

Instead of a nose,
Like the elephant's trunk,
It's a tongue underneath the butterfly's
   head.
It looks like a spring
Coiled up in a watch,
And it works like a streamer
You blow at a party.

If you follow a butterfly
Fluttering down
To gather the nectar
She finds in a flower,
You'll see how she stands
On the edge of a petal.

She suddenly shoots her rolled-up tongue
Into the cup of the flower.
The nectar she wants
Is down at the bottom,
And without her long tongue
She never could reach it.

How convenient!
Just like a soda straw.

THE FIREFLY

On a hot summer's night,
If you can't fall asleep,
Look out of your window and often you'll see
Hundreds of *Fireflies* flashing their lights.

No one's quite sure why Fireflies glow,
But we think it's the way
They call one another
At mating time.

The Firefly isn't a true fly at all;
It's really a soft-bodied beetle with wings.
The light it gives out
Doesn't come from its head;
It comes from its tail.
It's a cool light, a safe light;
It can't hurt you or burn.

In Japan
When they're giving a party at night,
The children go out on a Firefly hunt.
They gather big heaps of the bugs
While it's light,
For in daytime the Firefly's sleepy and
    slow.
They put them in lanterns,
They seal them up tight,
And when it gets dark
The lanterns all glow with the Fireflies'
    light.

It's a beautiful sight,
So gentle and cool on a hot summer night.

THE ANT

The first apartment house
In the whole wide world
Was built by the *Ants.*

They've been building their houses
For millions of years—
Not up in the air
But down in the ground.

If you lift up a stone
Or an old rotting log
There's a chance you will suddenly see
   them run wild.
They'll be rushing and pushing
In a terrible hurry
To carry their little white bundles to safety
   below.

Right under the stone,
Or the log which you lifted,
Is the roof of their house,
That is down in the earth.
It's a house of apartments—
A big house and deep.
There is floor upon floor and room after
   room,
With tunnels that lead from one room to
   another.
And they built it without ever making a
   sound.

The little white bundles are nests of new
   baby ants,
We call them cocoons.
And that's where they live
Until they grow up.
The ant nurses bring them upstairs
To be near the warm sun.
But if danger's about
They rush them to safety
Far down in the ground.

Most insects, we know,
Live alone by themselves.
But not so the ants;
They all live together.
They depend on each other
For help and for food,
For building their homes,
And protecting their young.
They each have their jobs
And they know what to do.

Some are workers,
Some are builders,
Some are soldiers.

Some can store up the food
In their bodies, like camels,
And can feed it to others
When food's hard to find.

Some even are farmers
Who keep insect cows
Known as *Aphids*
And milk them for juice.

And some are the nurses—
The smallest of all.
They take care of the babies
As soon as they're born.
They clean them and stroke them,
They feed and protect them
From the time they are eggs
Till the day they're full grown.

And then there's the queen;
She lays lots of eggs
And has hundreds of children.

The ants are worth watching
For there you can see
A little world all of its own.

THE TOAD

The *Toad* you will find
In your Tall Grass Zoo
Has a bug-catching tongue.
It's long and it's sticky.
It flips out so fast
That you hardly can see it.
And it laps up the bugs
As a cat laps up cream.

He's easy to find on a rainy day—
In the late afternoon,
Or the cool of the evening.
If he sees you he lies there
As still as a stone;
He pretends to be dead.

I wonder if you know
How a Toad takes a drink?
Not with his mouth,
But right through the pores
Of his bumpy brown skin.
That's why a Toad
Likes to walk in the rain.

THE SALAMANDER

Here's the spotted *Newt*,
Small and soft and pretty to look at.
She's also called a *Salamander*.

Pick her up.
Hold her on the flat of your hand.
How cold she is to the touch!
How full of fright!
Trembling, darting,
Not knowing which way to turn.

Better put her down.
Let her scurry away
Under the wet leaves,
Under the damp rocks
Where she makes her home.

The Newt is a creature who likes to be damp
Because she is born like a fish in the sea,
Hatched from an egg which is laid in the
   water.

At first she has gills
And breathes like a fish.
Her color is red, as bright as a berry.
We call her an *Eft* until she grows up.

Then she loses her gills.
She grows lungs instead.
She needs them in order to breathe on the land.
For two or three years she will live in the woods.
And her color will turn to a soft mossy green,
Sprinkled with spots of bright red on her back.
Then when she is ready to lay her own eggs
She'll go back to the water
In which she was born.

THE WOOLLY BEAR CATERPILLAR

It isn't a bear though it's got long hair.
It's not really a worm
For a worm won't turn
Like this one, into the moth *Isabella*.

It's a caterpillar called the *Woolly Bear*.

You'll find her in the autumn
When the leaves are beginning to turn.
Her color is black,
Striped with a band of reddish brown,
And she curls herself into a bristling ball
Whenever you touch her.

Some people think
That the Woolly Bear's band
Will tell you how cold
The winter is going to be.
The wider the band,
The milder the winter.
The thinner the band,
The more cold and snow.

Whichever it is,
The Woolly won't care
For she sleeps through the winter
In her thick, furry coat.

Then after the winter
In May, when it's spring,
She pokes her way out of her nest. . . .

What a change!

All the while she was sleeping
Inside her soft nest
Her body was turning from worm into
    moth.

Now she's lost all her hair.
She no longer crawls.
Her body's grown smaller
And sprouted soft wings.
Soon she'll spread out her wings
So they'll dry in the air.
Then away she will fly
And you'll see her at night,
In the summertime,
Beating her wings against the windowpane.

THE WOLF SPIDER

The *Wolf Spider* lives in the Tall Grass Zoo
And she is the one
Who carries her babies wherever she goes.

She keeps her eggs in a bag made of silk
Which she spins and then straps
Underneath her belly.

In the late summertime,
When the eggs have been hatched,
She cuts open the bag
With her sharp-edged jaws
And out pop the spiderlings—
Hundreds of them.
They scoot up their mother's eight long legs
Like cats up a tree.
They scramble and push
To find room on her back.
Then off they all go
To hunt for their dinner,
Swinging and swaying,
But holding on tight,
Like passengers on a crowded bus.

Some spiders spin webs to catch their prey,
But this one's a hunter.
She's fierce and she's strong,
And she moves with great speed.
That's why they call her the Wolf.

THE CLICK BEETLE

The Tall Grass Zoo has an acrobat
Who is called the *Click Beetle*
Because of the sound he makes when he
   jumps.

If he's turned on his back,
He doesn't lie helpless
As some beetles do,
Or like a turtle
Pawing the air with its legs.

He can do a neat trick;
It's a real acrobat's stunt.
He bends himself forward,
Then straightens up fast
With a snap and a click.
He leaps high in the air,
Turns head over heels,
And lands on his feet.

That's why some people call him the *Snap Jack*.

THE EARTHWORM

Here comes the *Earthworm*
Poking his head up out of the ground
While the night is still in the sky.

He'd better watch out
Or the early bird will get him.

Look at him closely
Before he burrows away into the earth.
He has no eyes and no ears,
But only a mouth.
And see how his body is made of rings—
Ring after ring in a long, long row,
And each of his rings is spiked with bristles—
Bristles so tiny they're hard to see
Without a magnifying glass.

The bristles are there to help him crawl.
He pushes them into the soil around him,
Then pulls himself along, ring by ring,
Like an acrobat climbing up a pole.

That's how the Earthworm does his work
Underneath the ground.

His work is helping the plants to grow
By burrowing through the ground,
By breaking up the soil
As you do with a rake,
By letting in air
And the rain and the seeds,
By swallowing the earth,
By bringing it up to the top of his hole,
By turning it over as you do with a spade.

In his quiet way
The squirming worm does all these things.
He may very well be
The hardest working gardener
In all the world.

THE LADYBUG

"Ladybug, ladybug, fly away home,
Your house is on fire, your children all
   gone;
All except one and that's little Ann,
And she has crept under the warming
   pan."

❋   ❋   ❋   ❋   ❋

That's the *Ladybug's* verse;
It's a very old rhyme.
You blow on the Ladybug gently and
   say it,
And then she'll fly off to the rescue,
   perhaps.
But it's not little Ann
She's going to rescue.

It's the fruit in the orchard she's going to
save.

It's the flowers your mother has grown in
her garden.

She saves them by eating the pests on the
leaves.

That's why the Ladybug is liked by the
farmer.

The pests would destroy all the fruit on
his trees.

But not when the Ladybug's there;

She's on guard!

She gobbles up pests as a mouse eats up
cheese.

THE PRAYING MANTIS

Three inches tall,
And as green as a leaf,
Or sometimes as brown as a twig in the fall.
She's hidden so well
That you can't always find her.
But once you have seen her
There's no doubt who she is.

Just see how she stands
As though saying a prayer!
That's why they call her the *Praying Mantis*.
Just look at her head
With its big searchlight eyes
Which can swivel around
So that nothing escapes her!

When she seems to be praying
She's lying in wait
For some careless insect to stray in her path.
She sits there so still
That they think she's a leaf.
But as soon as they're close
She will strike like a cat—
As quick and as sure.

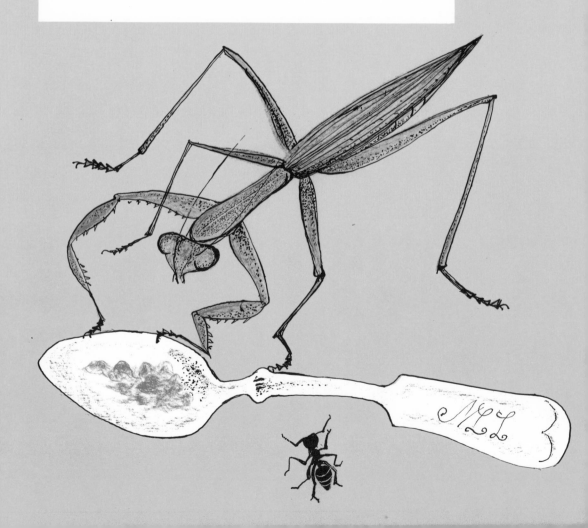

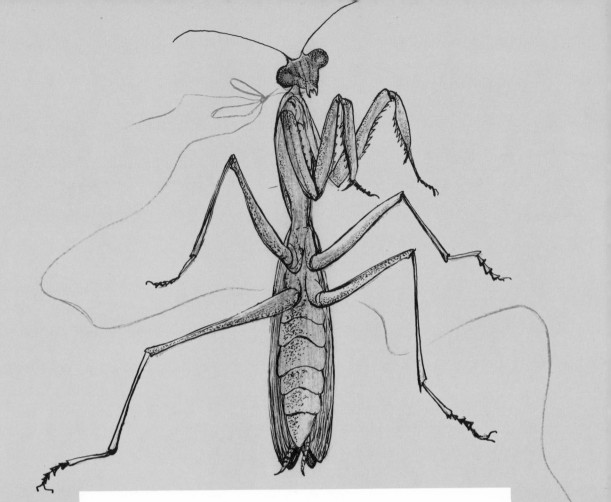

Yet, in spite of her fierceness,
She makes a fine pet.
She will walk on your hand.
She will sit in your hair.
You can put her on leash
With a thread round her neck.
She will eat bits of meat
And drink milk from a spoon.

In fact, she acts just as a house pet should.

THE SPITTLEBUG

A bird builds a nest,
A mole digs a hole,
A bee flies away to a honeycomb home.
But the insect I'm going to tell you about
Lives in a house made of lathery foam.

This is the insect we call *Spittlebug*,
But you also might call him
The Bubble-Bath Bug.
He squirts out a liquid
From the end of his body,
And whips it up into a big ball of suds,
As you do when you're making a bubble bath.

The first time you see these lathery houses
Clinging to leaves or to stalks in the grass,
You may think they are dew,
Or the juice from a plant.
But stroke down the froth,
Search through the foam,
And you'll find a small insect
With black pinhead eyes.

He's been sucking away at the sap in the
    grass.

He's only a baby, not ready to fly,
So he hides in the lather
Until he gets older.
When he's grown a hard skin,
And his wings have developed,
He'll be able to fly from his bubble-bath
    home.
Then we'll call him the *Froghopper*.

THE SNAIL

There are wonderful things about a *Snail*. . . .
His house is a shell;
That's easy to see
For he carries it with him
Wherever he goes.

He has only one foot
But it's big and it's flat.
He can use it to close up his house—
As you close your front door.
And with it he glides in his slow-moving
    way
Over prickly ground.
Through a jungle of grass,
Or straight up the side of a wall of glass.

The reason he's able to do all this
Is because, as he glides,
He puts out a gum that is sticky and wet.
It's a carpet to keep him from hurting his
    foot;
It's a trail you can follow to see where he's
    gone;
And it sticks him, like glue, to the side of
    the glass.

The snail has wonderful eyes, as well—
Two little black balls at the end of two
  horns.
They can turn and can twist;
He can see around a corner and over his
  head—
Like the periscope on a submarine.

If he loses an eye
The snail doesn't fret.
He grows on a new one as good as the
  old.
For him it's no worse
Than *you* getting a haircut or trimming
  your nails.

If he sees something coming,
He will pull in his horns,
And put out two feelers to guide him
  around.
But when he gets frightened,
He never takes chances—
He pulls in his feelers,
He shuts up his door,
And plays dead on the ground.

THE CICADA

Sometimes, in the summer,
If you hunt in your zoo,
You may find a brown shell
Sticking fast to a plant
Or a tree near the ground.

It *looks* like a bug,
But there's nothing inside.
It's the shell or the skin
Which belonged to an insect
We call the *Cicada*.

He's grown out of it now
In the same way as you
Grow out of your clothes.

This is the way the Cicada grows up:

First comes the egg
Which is tiny and white,
Laid by the mother in the bark of a twig.

Then out of the egg creeps the little Cicada.
It drops to the ground
And burrows away in the soil.

It stays underground for a very long time;

Sometimes as long as seventeen years.

In order to grow it must shed its old skin.
And it does this four times
While it's under the ground.
Each time that it sheds
It grows bigger and bigger,
Until it's full grown
And creeps up to the sun.

Now again the Cicada will shed its old skin
And this time—if you're lucky—
Perhaps you will see
How it changes itself
Right in front of your eyes. . . .

First it clings to a branch;
Then begins a long struggle
Inside the brown skin,
Which is now far too tight.
There's a pushing and heaving,
A stretching of muscles,
Until the old skin
Splits right down the back.

Inside you can see
A big soft green insect
Which is straining and wriggling
To get out of its shell.
It's not like the insect
Who lived underground.
Now it has wings.
At first they are wet
And cling to its body.
But soon it will spread out its wings
To dry in the air.

And then it will leave its old shell
Sticking fast to the branch.
It will fly far away.
You may hear its sad and whirring sound
High in the tree tops.

THE INSECT MUSICIANS

The *Grasshopper* is known
As an insect musician
Because of the music he makes
In the grass.

The sound you can hear
Doesn't come from his mouth.
It comes from his wings
Which he plays like a fiddle
By scraping and rubbing away
With his legs.

Those powerful legs
Are as strong as steel springs.
That's why he can jump
Right out of your hand,
And glide through the air
And land like a bird.

Zee—eee—eee—
That's the Grasshopper's sound.

There are two other insects
Very much like the Grasshopper.
But they make their music
By rubbing their wings,
One wing against the other.
One is the *Katydid*.
She's green, with long feelers,
Much longer than those
On the Grasshopper's head.
The sound she can make
Is a lot like her name—
Ka-ty-did. . . .Ka-ty-did. . . .

And there's also the *Cricket*,
Who is dark brown in color.
You sometimes can hear him
In winter
Down under the house.
He makes bright little sounds
Like a chirruping whistle,
Going *chirr-p*,
And *chirr-p*,
And *chirr-p*.